CW01497851

All poems by Wynn D. Day
Front Cover photograph by Kevin Masterson

More
64^Eclectic Poems for a Windy Day

by Wynn D. Day

Contents

AN EVERYDAY SIXTIES GIRL

It's hard to wear stilettos
As she staggers down the bus,
She wants to make it to the top
So she doesn't make a fuss.

With her buttoned up cardy,
And conical bra,
And her pencil pleated skirt,
She's bound to go far.

She's travelling to the office,
And she needs to be on time.
She jumps down from the bus
Then up the steps she climbs.

She hastens in and eyes the clock,
It's just gone half past eight,
She hurries to her typewriter,
The manager glares – she's late.

Next, her boss calls her in,
It's time for some dictation.
And with her shorthand pencil poised,
She waits for his oration.

He looks across at her crossed legs,
At her stockings tan and sheer.
She sees his eyes peruse their shape,
Then pats his lap. "Come here."

She knows that this is how it is,
In these early sixties days.
If you want to make it to the top,
You walk along these ways.

She sits upon his bumpy knee;
She feels his stinking breath.
He runs his hand along her leg –
It makes her wish for death.

Is this really how it is?
To make something of yourself,
To a slimy man you give your body
For the sake of making pelf!

She knows it's wrong. She moves away.
She sees his startled look.
She hurries out. She shuts the door,
And leaves her shorthand book.

Humiliated, she gets her things,
Hangs her head as she leaves.
The others in the office watch
As she wipes her nose on her sleeve.

Confused, she thinks, there must be a way
For a girl to earn a living.
A way for her to earn her pay
So her soul she won't be giving.

She thinks about the boy next door,
Who wants her for his wife.
Is that the only way that she
Can make something of her life?

The choice is stark. She can either be
A wife and mother or whore,
But in these so restrictive times
She's wrong – if she thinks there's more.

MUMMY KNOWS BEST

Have you heard the latest fashion,
For getting your nose knocked off?
It's supposed to be quite painless
Then they throw it in a trough.

It really is death enhancing,
And it means that they never can tell
Exactly where you came from,
But you do lose the power of smell.

You sometimes may find me posing,
At the fair, as a coconut shy.
People throw wooden balls at my hooter,
As they are meandering by.

It's such a glorious feeling,
As it falls to the floor.
The wonderful sound of it cracking
Makes me want it more and more.

We happy band of mummies,
With our faces all deformed,
Want to get the message right across
So everyone is reformed.

This look is now so classical,
It's how everyone should be.
Go and get your nose shot off
And you can be just like me!

DECEMBER SONG

Twilight hurried across the firmament.
The ghost of the sky was cold.
He lay down and pulled
A pink grey cloud about him
To sleep.

The December afternoon was old
And inviting chilly dusk
To stalk empty lanes
Where loneliness wraps around
Naked trees.

Congealed mist concealed misery,
Looking out for victims –
Forgotten winter souls –
Denuded of breath and spirit,
Deo favento.

Quiesent, save for the whisper of hope,
When the solstice breaks the spell
Of baleful hidden light,
And the guiding star shall rise
In excelsis.

WELSH SHARK

It came upon the eighth day,
A denizen from the deep.
Sharp glistening golden teeth,
A gourmet harvest to reap.
By mischance, it came my way.

But when'ere I wished it away,
It aimed to be like water.
Poison coursed through its aorta –
Golden toothed to the slaughter!
So sure that this would be its day.

"Come with me, come away – come away,
You'll be entranced with my notions!
For massage and miraculous potions
I take the essence from the oceans,
Upon this sacrilegious day."

POP

Back in the sixties when I was a kid
We had yummy Corona pop.
When all kids were dizzy this pop was fizzy
And bought from the grocer's shop.

At school we'd learn - with no concern -
Corona was a crown.
We couldn't care much, it wasn't as such
The word could be more than a noun.

Our biology broke the mythology
Coronary was a heart attack!
This was a bummer to awaken the dumber
Let's have the old days back!

Orange pop to drink we'd never think
Of the meanings and all such stuff.
Now out of China comes the opiner
A Corona will kill us all off!

(Written during the pandemic of 2020)

THE WISH OF SOMNOLENCE

6am. Now.
Two hours of enforced wakefulness.
Aching body,
Sickness advancing,
And sleep, eluding my efforts
To catch it.
It plays hide and seek.
I desire it more than anything –
But it's evil face
Sneers and sniggers
As my desperation calls to it.
Every movement is painful;
Most painful of all
Is my demonised brain,
Invaded and overrun.
I feel helpless –
Victimised – I did not want this
"It was someone else's fault!"
I should have stayed sleeping
Except for the movement of another body
And now I have this hell.
This place is on the edge of life
Where sneaking sleep
And marauding demons
Circle like vultures
Tormenting me
With exasperated sourness
And lassitude.
I long for sleep.

THRENODY

My weary footsteps took me far,
And eager now for sleep
I sought a berth to rest myself
Somewhere that I might creep;
To take a rest to end all rests
With slumbers leaden deep.

I let my eyes traverse the ground
And there my gaze was led
To a bed of bella donna –
A place to lay my head.

So soft and sweet her leaves
Around my face did twine,
With perfumes mellowed in the woods
And laced with sweet woodbine.

The seed heads rocked my worn-out soul
As I sought no space or time.
Upon my hallucinatory path
Gehenna stole my mind.

And Judah's babes reached out to me
Reaching through the fire.
Grasping fingers appealing to me
Watching me through the pyre.

"Oh no" I cried, "This cannot be,
What madman's reign is here?
To suck the life from these poor babes
To let them die in fear?"

I turned away from the wicked sight
So great was my despair.
I cursed my need for mescaline
And its power to ensnare.

The cries of haunted children
Are buried in my brain.
Mescaline with its evil strands
Has made my world insane.

MR HEAD AND HIS HAT

Mr Head goes to the shop
To buy himself a hat.
He's not too sure about the fit
But he's not worrying about that!

He puts it on, and down it goes
And covers up his eyes.
In the breeze he lifts it up
And with a heavy gust it flies

Away it goes, across the road
As on the wind it spun.
A group of mice then pick it up,
And down the road they run.

With four and twenty legs astride,
They go hell for leather.
A grey goose flying overhead
Looks for cover from the weather.

"Ah, there's the thing," he soon decides,
And dive bombs down to earth.
He swoops majestically and takes the hat
From six mice running for all they're worth.

He flicks it round upon his head
But knows it's not his style.
It's a useful cover against the rain
He'll keep it for a while.

And when the sun comes shining through
He tips it to the ground.
A brown bear dancing in the woods
Thinks, "Look at what I've found!"

It fits just right on his big head,
And his dance gets very jiggy,
And everyone admires his hat
Then it's stolen by a piggy.

"Oi, give it back," the brown bear shouts,
As he chases down the road.
The pig runs off out of sight,
Then he gives it to the toad.

"I like this hat," says Mr Toad
"I'll use it for a boat."
He gets his oars and off he goes
But finds that it won't float.

He clambers up the river bank,
And as the hat sinks down,
A pike comes swimming underneath
And takes it as his crown.

"Oh, this will suit me very well,"
And his jaws snap left and right.
And all the little fishes flee
As he glides into the night.

And next day as the sun comes up,
Mr Head is going fishing.
It starts to rain, he's getting wet
And it's for his hat he's wishing.

And as the hours drift slowly by,
The float moves round and round.
As Mr Head whips out the line
His hat falls on the ground.

Misshapen, wet and slimy green
He eyes it with disgust.
But now the rain is pelting down
But on his head he must…

Refit the hat – cause now it's shrunk
All hung around with slime.
He doesn't care, and then proclaims,
I've got it back – it's mine!"

THE AUCTION

"What am I bid? What am I bid?"
The auctioneer hammering cried.
"For this double fronted house
With the well-known Claverdon brook
Traversing by its side.

47 acres, 0 roods and 11 perches –
Known as the Old Mill Farm.
Valuable, small and well-watered.
And for those who have seen it – you'll agree –
A place of great charm.

It is let on Michaelmas tenancies
To Mr Inglis, Margetts and Moore.
And Mr Moore pay a pound for the
Sheep wash, which is situated
by the back door.

With entrances, porches and bedrooms,
Excellent water from the well.
There are useful brick-built farm buildings
For cows, horses, hens and a piggery –
But please watch out for the smell!

There is also a tiled and brick weigh office,
In the field next to Claverdon Road.
With valuable tithes and land taxes,
And timber valued at £248 8s 9d –
Surely a very big load!

Sporting rights let to Messrs. Galton and Margetts.
(They go shooting down there every day),
With an area of over 47 acres.
A place with pasture aplenty, and much room
For people to play.

In field number 433, .675 acres –
This plot to the railway was sold,
But now it's rented from Great Western Railway
By Mr Margetts for fifteen bob.
This lot is freehold.

Now Come gentlemen, what am I bid
For these wonderful parcels of land?
Do I hear five hundred and fifty guineas?
Yes. Out there from Mr Addenbrooke.
Sold. And this bid shall stand.

FLOWER CHANT

A mystic breeze blows through the fronds
Awakening faeries long asleep,
And off they creep towards the ponds
And meadows dark and deep.

They form a roundel – oh so sweet,
And in their pretty dance,
They pick astrantia small and neat
To guarantee romance.

Then off they fly to find the one
Their spell to then impart,
And with a posy of mezereon
Will captivate their heart.

On a sleeping girl in a pretty dress
They lay their posy down,
And cover her in pennycress,
And then go to search the town

To find a boy for her to meet
With a fritillary of flowers,
And set his youthful heart to beat,
To while away the hours…

Sitting upon banks of saxifrage
With lover's songs to float,
They waft in waters upon their barge
To the sound of the pardilote.

Then off together the chosen pair –
Their hands a perfect link,
From the meadow floor pick dittander
To the song of the bobolink.

And in the meadow now they dwell
Below the blossomed tree,
So happy in their faerie spell
In the land of the picotee.

STOLEN DREAMS

In the night, in the dark,
The sandman scattered
Steps in her mind to
Lead to her dreams.
Airy, floating, soft
And distant.
Comfortable in repose
They flitted and shone.

From the night, from the dark,
A thief crept by
And saw the shining dreams.
He stared and sneaked
And stole her soul.
The airy dreams
He took and fled.

And in the night, and in the dark,
She stares in silence
As a sinister nightmare
Takes place before her eyes.
She knows the thief - who sneaks and steals
The lives and souls
Of those who dream.

ADVENT-ITIOUS

Well. Go on then.
It's there for you to climb.
Like the ivy that clings to it,
Around and upwards.
You think you should be accompanied?
Well. A pinch of ginger –
That helps.
And garlic. With spits and spots of
Raindrops. Soft. Like a Spring dawn,
And you close your eyes
And feel it.
And you want it forever…
But no. It doesn't last.
You have a ladder.
That's right,
It's easy after you get started.
What's that?
You wish it was Jacob instead.
No, this is your opportunity; your chance.
There's no point in thinking.
You can't come back.
You have to keep going up.
You shouldn't have got in the way.
It's no use complaining.
You're dead now.
Just go on.
You see a spiral?
Ah. Now that's a good sign.
Feathers. Like a white swan,
Yes. Downy, soft, with kind faces
That'll be…
Well, you know now.

WALKING THE PLAGE DE L'ABER

My feet kick at the sheer shimmering water.
It creates my breathtaking reply of pleasure,
And tingling, reverberating joy.
Tiny fish dart in tiny wavelets
Changing colour at every turn of the sun's shadow.
A path of scattered shells beckons ever onwards.
Constellations of starfish lie along the shoreline
With grasping minute tentacles.
Tight yellow muscle shells – showing two pincers for victory –
Burrow into the wet sand and disappear.
Tiny hermit crabs in stolen homes
Roll back and forth in the surf –
Some joined and rolling fifth, sixth and seventh…
At the beaches end – in the rock pool,
Lies the King of starfish.
Its encrusted arms shifted by heavy waves
As if to dictate its temporary reign
While on show to the world.
And the sea lives at my side
Sending bubbly wavelets to issue their wares to the shore,
To lie hidden or to die on the sand
Until the sea returns by command of the moon god.

OXALIC CILAXO

A cluster closely conjured up
Beside a silver stream,
Where lay a poisoned chalice
Which flowed into a dream.

And through its wafting tendrils
There gazed two sunken eyes,
Which glistened in the spangled pool
With all of dead men's lies.

Salted crystalline, acid sharp
The poisoned lake turned back,
And opened up ratafia swirls
With curls of putrid black.

Then faster on and faster
The venom did its work
To the jaws of hidden monsters
Where in the depths did lurk –

Fetid stinking rat's bones,
The kind that make you shake,
And bums so big with pimples
And great big plates of steak.

If you have any reason
To think this makes some sense,
I hope you're not offended
'Cause it's all a big pretence!

VERTIGO

Weaving a waft of wonderment,
Spinning around and around,
Gardens of ghostly glauconites,
The best that can ever be found.

Mountains of mesmering minerals,
Spinning around and around,
Quadrants of quartzy quadrupoles,
All making a beautiful sound.

Uranium uplands and uvarovites,
Spinning around and around,
Charming and churning and chapfallen,
Spreading themselves on the ground.

Sucking silvery silicon silicates,
Spinning around and around,
Flitting fairies and frogs fanfaronade,
And vertiginous sickness abounds.

This fantasy world starts to tumble,
Spinning around and around.
And disintegrates into a fairyland,
And disappears under a mound.

FOR FRANCES

Let's have a party –
Let's have a party in the past.
Let's go to a place before we knew,
When we sat at desks to listen
And then to gather and gossip.
Let's find our friends
And take their hands.
Let's be young, let's be there.

The wizened women
Hesitate… "Do I remember you?"
"Oh yes…"
But their hands are no longer soft
Now they have brown spots
And lumpy veins.
Their look is no longer innocent
And their memories do not go
To the exact places…
Their feelings for that past time
Seem not to exist…

But there is someone –
Someone who would know.
She would feel like me
She would understand.

But when I look,
When I find her footsteps
They do not lead where they should.
Here is her home,
It's foundations falling
Its wood filled with worms
Whose powder drizzles downwards…
Through the gaping roof
Dust twizzles in the sunlight.
Here is her eternity.

No party now for the memories.
No laughter or mirth.
Just the silence of my footsteps
To her cavern of sleep.

SNORKELLING

The cool, clear world beneath me
Lies full
Of crazy cosmopolitan serenity
Wafting colours,
Little fins propelling
Lives here and there.
The only sound is my rhythmic breath
Breaking the underwater silence.
A ray of sunlight
Sends sheaths and circular shafts
To unending depths,
Bypassing knotty columns of corals
That stand erect as towers
For hungry bypassers to nibble.
Fine hairy fronds
Lift lightly with the passing current.
Startling colours drift before my eyes.
Vivid royal blue
With a staring egg yolk eye upon its belly,
And its owner sucks the reef
And passes on
To be replaced with
Gay carnivals stripes of dusky pink
And apple green, and bright canary yellow.
More and more, big and little.
A golden shoal
Swims beside the sunbeam,
And above them
Lies a host of electric blue microcosms
Darting hither and thither
In the surface sunshine.
Great was my joy
At the sights in this aquatic garden.

PLAYTIME FOR THE YOUTH 2005

He gazes intently at the screen.
His eyes dart
From one murderous victim
To the next.
His fingers move animatedly
On the plastic buttons.
He contorts the fate
Of virtual murder
Before his darting eyes.

His thumbs become still.
His virtual victims hang
In timeless tragedy.
He takes another swig.
The alcohol pummels his brain again,
And his eyes glaze with moisture.
He takes another. And another.
Till his soaked mind
Dances with suspended murderers.
He sleeps.
His lonely dreams
Circle a virtual beauty
Who robotically speaks
Words of computerised comfort.
She stops.
In suspended silence
Her meaningless gaze
Churns his beating brain.
He reaches out.
His glassy eyes open
To his den of solitude.
He watches the silence
The constant nothingness
The unthinking mind
The spectre of unending lonliness…

MORRIGAN

The foe is vanquished, the victor fled.
The carrion scavengers hover around the dead.

In this land of broken dreams,
Though I must obey Morrigan, I am not what I seem.

I promised Morrigan I would walk away,
But I see your face and know you have to pay.
And I'm not ready to go without a fight,
Though I know that Morrigan forbids that right.
And I must leave and not look back.
But now, (like Lots wife, but with my stone so black,)
I will collect my pride and make as if to go,
But deep inside my wretched heart I know
I cannot let your life continue on,
So when your back is turned my stone becomes weapon.

I hurl it at your head. You fall to the ground dead.

But Morrigan is just, and there is no escape for me.
And now her ravens will never let me be…

Think not to thwart a Goddess so fair,
For by Morrigans hand she deals justice so rare.

And soon I know my time will come,
And by Morrigans hand thy will be done.

UNCERTIFIED

Where am I and what am I now?
Yet for five hours I have failed to draw breath
And my blood has ceased its traverse.
Cold and still I lie,
But in this place, this time
-Without the official acknowledgement-
I am free to be
Within the world or without it.
My spirit still has licence to dance a jig,
For no pronouncement has been the judge
Of whether I still have a place of existence.
Without a civilised earthly decision
I still have the rights of those who live and breathe.
Lacking this certainty,
I may still look back to view the path I travelled
And feel that lightness of heart
As I smell the air and hear the birdsong.
But soon my maker will beckon –
When proper permission is granted
For me to make my way to
Well…
Where I shall be and what I shall be then!

DOT.COM.SLASH.

Suppose Dot would come?
Let us see Dot and Com
At the ball.
Elegantly Dot. dances,
But not with a slash
   with a sash.
See she glides.
See Dot's dainty feet
As she twirls and glides
And her sash
Not her slash
Swirls, as a carousel.
Dot and Com
Round they go
   Faster Faster
And her sash
Not her slash
Gets entwined
As she glides
    And it pulls
    And it pulls
    Tighter.
Her sash
Not her slash -
Not the slash of a blade
As it pierces
But a sash –
A harmless old sash –
Not a slash as it murders,
But a sash as it strangles.

ALLISSIA'S SMILE

Like a dish of plum coloured cherries
Waiting for their taste to be savoured,
Sits my little girl
Swinging in the soft warm sun.
Emerging innocence from babyhood.
Her pretty face
And dark Caribbean eyes
Seek surety
From those around who love her.
She catches my blessed gaze,
And exchanges a smile with me
So large and pure
It spreads joyous contagion,
And conveys a secret message
That only Nan and well-loved baby
Can understand.
My precious gift;
As perfect as plump peaches,
And delicious as dairy ice cream,
In the early summer sunshine.

RAINDROPS

She could have sold a rainbow
And split it all apart,
She could have sold a journey
And truly lost her heart.
She could have sold the setting sun
Its gilded rays so hot,
But she wanted to sell raindrops
The kind that never stop.

She could have sold the words they said
But let them fall away.
She could have sold the steps she took
But saved them for the day
When she sold her soul to heaven
To look down from the top,
But she wanted to sell raindrops
The kind that never stop.

She wants to buy a landscape
To sit and drink the view.
She wants to buy another world
'Cause this one just won't do.
She wants to find a fiery mass
Her troubles there to drop,
And that will end the raindrops
The kind that never stop.

POPPIES

The warm summer English breeze
Blew the poppies in the hedgerows.
These sweet gentle ripples
Belie the saddest day
When I knew my friend would not return.
We had shared stories
Of babies, of places we knew,
Of doing our best for the sick.
"I'm going to war
To the land of the Poppies."
"Why go?"
"I took the money.
I am a man of honour.
I am a soldier."
My blood shivered.
He would be back. He promised.

The blind politician's battle
Backfired for the kill –
For the taking
Of the father of babies.
The cateracted eyes
Look to the English poppies
And think of him fallen
In the cause of the vermillion flower.
And a soft voice for Richard says:
"Forgive them Father
For they know not what they do."

COMPANION

Misery loves company
In fact, he came my way.
"What are you doing tomorrow
Or indeed, what are you doing today?

I've got a lousy feeling
That I'd really like to share
You look like the type of person
Who seems to really care.

I know it may seem obvious
From the look upon my face,
That I have this sinking feeling
And I'm sure that it's a case

Of too much negative thinking
As my evil thoughts accrue.
I'm sure you're the guy who'll help me
And tell me what to do."

I shrugged and hurried onwards,
But then he grabbed my arm.
I pushed his grubby hand away
And looked at him with alarm.

"Look, will you just get lost mate?
I have better things to do
Than hanging round street corners
Being chased by the likes of you!"

I immediately felt so sorry
For the harsh words I had said.
I saw tears standing in his eyes –
This situation I'd misread.

It seemed he needed comfort –
Someone to help him on his way,
So we made our way to a park bench
And I said, "What's up with you today?"

His words spilled out like water,
His tone deadly as the grave.
It seemed he'd done some misdeed,
Then his sobs they came in waves.

He begged for me to hide the gun
And keep it somewhere safe.
I recoiled from him in horror
But I was locked in his embrace.

He took me to a prison
When he wrapped his arms so tight.
Now my world is full of demons
As I gaze into the night.

The gun has now become a noose
As it drags me to my knees.
This misery has caused my world to end
And my gentle heart to freeze.

THE STONE MAN

The stone man looks to his empty bowl.
His cold stone heart
As empty as his bowl.
He has stood for aeons,
And has seen the world
And felt his feeling sinter
Through time.
Once he thought the world a good place,
He was optimistic in his reason;
But he watched
And tears fell from his glassy eyes
As sadness gathered around him.
He has seen his bowl fill with dust
And empty promises.
He has heard angry voices
And cries of pain,
And he has felt the rain –
Not the sweet rain to nourish the sacred earth –
But cold sharp rods of steel
As they pierced his body.
He stands eremitic
And wishes.
He wishes for soft sustenance
To fill his bowl
For his friends the birds.

THE NIBBLE IN THE KIBBLE OF QUIBBLE AND SCRIBBLE

Quibble and Scribble
Lived in a kibble,
And dribbled
All over everyone
As they were hoisted
Heavenward -
In their kibble.
They would nibble
As they fribbled
And dribbled
In their kibble.
But they quibbled
As they anticipated
Their meeting
With Saint Peter.
As they quibbled
In their kibble
They scribbled
A note
In anticipation.
And they quibbled
Over who would nibble
And dribble
In the kibble
When they got there.
Quibble scribbled
On Scribble.
Scribble dribbled
On Quibble,
And they nibbled
And dribbled
As they went to heaven.

A VIEW FOR VENUS

Venus lay in her blue heaven.
The west wind was prowling
Inciting the cloud to cover her face.
It pulsated. It shimmied.
It seemed reluctant.
The west wind insisted on its compliance,
"Cover her. Cover her," he spat.
But the cloud approached in awe.
It weaved, and tried to disperse
And then thinly spread itself
Like a veil.
So Venus still reigned supremely,
And gazed out from her netted sheen
To watch her sister Earth
And all the foolish beings upon it.

THE GIMLET TREE

My love lay beneath the tree with the twist,
But my feelings I thought, were just an illusion,
And I felt my love die, fading with the mist.
Her blood red lips I had kissed
And my mixed up feelings – just confusion.
My love lay beneath the tree with the twist;
I decided then to end our tryst
But she declared her love in profusion,
But I felt my love die – fading with the mist.
I begged her over, please to desist.
It was then there was an intrusion.
My love lay beneath the tree with the twist
And an assassin struck her with his fist,
He brought her life to its conclusion,
And I felt my love die, fading with the mist.
I ran fast, his murderous mind to resist,
And I left my love dead, in Azraeled seclusion.
My love lay beneath the tree with the twist,
And I felt my love die – fading with the mist.

STILL SHE SAT IN HER CHAIR

In those days, when she could,
She had eaten –and eaten- what she would.
And she grew fat – as she should,
But she knew it did her absolutely no good.

When she grew old and sat in her chair –
In her second floor flat, living where
She was comfortable – she had everything there,
But old age brought a new set of care.

She grew sick and they said she should
Call the doctor who said that she would
Go to hospital, so that they could
Sort her out, and make it once again all good.

And when the ambulance got there,
They moved her to the doorway where
It was too narrow for her chair,
So they couldn't even reach the stair!

They called an expert who said they should
Bring in a crane so it could
Lift the roof off so that they would
Get her out of there – (that would be good.)

And then they hoisted her into the air,
And still she sat upon her chair.
Perhaps she was well stuck in there –
Then off to hospital – with great flair!

CATALYTIC CATBURGLAR

Tyger Brown has lots of cats,
They cost so much to feed.
He had to find a way so that
He could buy food to keep them fat
He was amazed how fast they'd breed!

The day when he ran out of cash,
'Twas when he made a plan.
A burglar he'd be – with panache,
From smart cars he'd make a stash,
And be the catalytic converter man.

He donned a mask and sack so black,
And stepped into the night.
And with his saw upon his back
He found a car along a track,
With its cat-con shining bright.

He fumbled round and got his saw,
His torch began to flicker.
He sawed and sawed – twas quite a chore,
But then he saw feet upon the floor,
And then he saw the vicar!

He knelt beside him on the ground.
"Now what are you doing here?
You're doing that wrong – I'll be bound.
Move over – where's the space to be found?
You'll be here all night I fear."

The vicar gently prised the prize
All full of precious metal.
"Now. This deal we should finalise.
This one's for me. I apologise
But that is how I'll settle."

But Tyger punched him on the nose
And down the road he ran.
"Come back," the vicar bellows.
But Tyger's off – the cat enclosed –
He jumped into his van.

THE TENDERNESS COMPETITION

Upon a green field far away,
The little veggies gather.
Eager to compete on their special day,
All getting in a lather.

Up in the blue and cloudless sky,
The warming sun shone down,
To greet the judges who are nigh,
All coming from the town.

The swede, the broad bean and the pea
All take a lofty seat,
And need the shade of the chestnut tree
To keep them from the heat.

The little veggies, neat and small,
All anxious for the crown,
Begin to sweat and then to bawl,
And some of them turn brown.

"We need a place where we can hide
From the sizzly sun so hot.
We'll be no use, we will be fried,
And no good for you lot!"

"I'm getting tough," a young pea said.
"I cannot stand much more.
I feel a pain coming in my head."
Then fell promptly to the floor.

The other veggies looked around,
Their consternation growing.
How could they be judged upon the mound?
There was no way of knowing.

The tender veggies, small and sweet,
All sitting in the sun.
The swelled and popped all in the heat
Before the judging begun.

"Well, that's no good," began the judge,
As he watched the veggies popping.
"The Bird's Eye men will bear a grudge;
They'll be no good in the shopping!"

The judges wearily wondered off
And left the toughened veggies,
All lying, dying with a cough,
And fraying round the edges.

The moral of this story is,
To keep your veggies tender.
Don't let them go in competitions –
Keep them in the fridge!

STARS

On the wayside bank
Lie stars growing.
They nestle in the mosses
Growing and glowing
As they practice
For their spangled show
On Christmas Eve.
On this hot July afternoon
They seem to know their future task,
To guide three wise men
Hurrying to Bethlehem
Following a leading silver star,
Which will grow a beautiful shining tail
To help them on their way.
For now, they lie on their bed of moss
And bask in the warm afternoon sun.

MY NEW FRIEND

Welcome to my new friend Amiante.
Introduced to me by an associate,
And assured of her integrity.
She stands stiff and proud,
Not really welcoming
But I am assured of her genuine nature –
And of her endurance.
But she will not meet my eye,
And her breath smells –
Intoxicatingly.
Her touch, is like grainy cotton wool
Which leaves a trail on my skin
And her fingers linger on me
When they should have withdrawn
And they…
But she has a strange attractiveness;
I feel drawn to her.
After all, she has such a pretty French name.
Amiante. Amiante.
Half of it friend – Ami.
Now she looks my way
And my throat starts to tighten.
And my breathing becomes constricted.
And my head grows light,
And the truth of her pretty name
Discloses itself.
Amiante – handmaiden of asbestos.

ODE TO THE EAST WIND

The spiteful wind with bitter breath,
Penetrates needles through cheeks.
His chilled Siberian cousins
Blow cutting kisses
To help him on his way.

Ribboned snowflakes waft on the air
Driven through the distance
By the evil east wind.
Like a sniper
Eager to show his power-
To show his warlike prowess,
He seeks his targets.
He spits to cut-
To slice with blades of icy wrath.

But he has no enemy,
Save the warming summer sun.
He seeks no revenge.
He just likes to wait
In the bleak forests
With his cold cousins
For a surprise attack,
When he shall set out again
To kill with cruelty;
To pierce the flesh of his victims
With the lash of his gelid tongues.

PAINTBRUSH

After her hard mornings work
She lay wet. At rest.
Her beautiful skirt now neutral,
Devoid of the lovely colours
-her gay apparel of the matin.
How his hands had made her dance!
Her skirt, rich with paint,
Twisted and turned
As it glided over the vapid gaps.
It dipped again
And then swirled and twirled
Beneath his deft fingers.
How great was her joy
As the movement melody
Changed the surface it played on
To happy, harmonious colour.
Backwards and forwards she fled,
And her merry labours
Became a thing of beauty.
On and on…
Until it became time to rest.
She longs for the morrow
When once more
She will rapturously toil and frolic.

THUNDERSTORM

The night and the thunder
Jockeyed for the services of the dark.
"He is mine by right," said the night
"Nature decreed him to me."
"I cannot function properly without him."
 Said the thunder.
"And anyway, my companion-
The lightening,
Is married to him.
You cannot have dark without light
Or the world will not function."
Night was contemptuous.
"I join the light and dark together quietly
On every day that passes.
You come around in Summertime
Creating a din to shake heaven –
And cast terror into the people,
And pass it off as an excuse
For hot and cold air meeting;
And you demand the services of my darkness!
It is not good enough."
"I began the world.
My electrical forces
Stimulated the very life
You claim to organize every day."
"Pish." Flashed the wayward lightening.
"Come away with me thunder.
Let us go and make love
Wherever we choose
And let everyone know about it!"

DEATH BREATH

My journey draws forward through an eerie chalk drawing;
Smudged distant lights,
Then flying veils of icy, fine sugar strands
On this late winter night
Moving into the relentless, debilitating cold.

The death breath wind
Changes fronds of winter grass
Into a skeletal hand
That haplessly grasps the ground.

Snowdrifts, with soft folds of wynciette
Lie scattered carelessly beside the highway.
Pouting, windy lips blow its surfaces.

A whispered command;
An exodus of snow – chased to the slaughter.

White minutiae, like airborne lace tablecloths
Are tossed around at evil will.
Christmas come late with menace.

(Beast from the East - 2018)

CORNWALL'S WINTER AFTERNOON

Dusk is calling
Celsius falling
Murmuring in the sky.
Starlings winging wide and high
Come to see the daylight die.

Gilded sky – a perfect pink.
Down towards the night we sink.
And watching Cornwall's stricken brow
In winter's grip, we wonder how
We honoured summer, when we see her now!

BONG

Listen up guys, this is it
I've got a spanking piece of kit.
Now if I want to go anywhere
My new satnav will get me there.
As down the country lanes I wend,
It tells me all about the bend.
And when I get into a town
Knives and forks are scattered around,
Indicating places for eating out,
And fine dining – that's what it's all about.
And there's a function that's really cool,
It tells me where to get my fuel.
And bong, when you're speeding,
And bong when you're feeding
(Cause you know it's wrong.)
And bong to spoil your song.
In fact it bongs so much
It gets on your nerves, such
A menace – it becomes a bonging
Machine. Bonging, bonging, bonging –
I think I'll turn it off.

LILAC

I look inside the soul of the lilac
And see its story from long ago.
In the delicate perfection of petals
I see a face
Radiating love and joy.
Its contours
Follow the lines
Of nature's bounty
As she looks back at me
And smiles.
A re-creation of lost days
When our world was cozy
And filled with posies of love
And laughter
And words of common interest.
Shared pleasures with my granny,
As the soft spring winds
Blew around our world;
And we nestled
Into the loving comfort
Of her lilac scented room.

VIRGIN

I am a virgin pure and proud,
Sex –for me- is not allowed.
My hymen is said to haunt men's dreams,
And is the source of many schemes.
It is an honour for me to keep,
Until I yield it for love so sweet.
My innocence and child-like state,
Belie the blossoming desire of fate -
To be seduced by a would be lover
Who makes me think there is no other.
Or if it's stolen – poached by rape,
It would be ended – no escape.
I keep it safe, at my discretion,
My state of grace - my prize possession.
So all you men who wish to be
In my bed and next to me;
It may not be hard to pop a cherry,
Be true to me and make me merry.

FAT ROLL CHAT

We're invited in at Christmas,
When we come to join the fun.
The first place that we head for
Is to gather round your bum.

We see you eye the table
Filled with calories galore,
And just because it's Christmas
You'll always take one more.

Tis the season to be merry –
An excuse to have a drink.
You tip them back with festive glee
And you never have to think

Just what will be the outcome,
As you try to fit your pants.
You struggle as you pull them up,
And then you find you can't.

We form a lovely cushion
And I think we're here to stay.
You keep piling all the food in
It really makes our day.

For your New Year's resolution
You decide we have to go.
But you're buying lots of smocks
To make sure that we don't show.

We sit in folds around your waist,
And when it comes to Spring,
You think your fat looks so bad
You really must do something.

You buy some jogging bottoms –
The biggest you can get –
And by the end of the road
You're building quite a sweat.

But this is very painful
As you flop us all about.
It makes us all begin to cry
Our future is in doubt!

You've bought a new bikini,
As skimpy as can be.
This really does look worrying
It could be the end of me!

And flip, flip, flip, flop, flop, flop,
And now we're at the gym.
I just can't stop my crying
As this body's getting thin.

And as you keep on jumping,
I hear the trainer say,
"Sweat means your fat is crying."
Could this be my last day?

THE TORIES SLOPPING OUT

Brace yourself – it's chaos!
The country's in a spin.
But we're chained to a lunatic
And no-one's going to win.

And if you choose to grow old,
And no one seems to care,
Cause you're chained to a lunatic
They'll say you've had your share.

If you sail across on a boat
Because you want to live here,
You'll be chained to a lunatic –
Be sure you'll find no cheer.

Now we're off to the food bank,
To endure this shameful stint.
We're chained to a lunatic
Cause now everybody's skint.

And with fuel prices high
And everyone's on strike,
Cause we're chained to a lunatic
We have to use our bike.

And when the currency collapsed
For the Bank of England's boss,
Cause we're chained to a lunatic
It became the people's loss.

When Liz Truss lost our trust
She caused a money hole,
Cause we're chained to a lunatic
It created a bigger toll.

And MPs want to be celebs
And go into the jungle,
We are chained to this lunatic
Something else for him to bungle.

If anyone wants to be PM
And visit this slippery place,
They'll be chained to a lunatic
And surely fall on their face.

Now this lot has us puzzled,
How do we put this right?
As we're chained to this lunatic
How can we win this fight?

(November 2022)

THE LEAPING SPIDER

I'm the incy wincy spider
Living on the door,
And if it wasn't for all the noise
I'd be living there some more!

I was sitting quietly
In my web catching prey,
Till this big black wet thing
Quite upset my day.

Woof, woof, woof, bark, bark, bark –
It nearly deafened me.
It was just so upsetting
I felt I had to flee.

I leaped away up high,
From my cosy bed,
And landed under the cabinet
Where I bumped my head.

It's really dark down here,
I can't see the sun.
When I lived on the door
The afternoons were fun.

I could do my sunbathing;
But through that pesky dog,
I find myself stuck down here –
It's like being in the fog.

I really want to go back home,
And live on the front door.
It's such a sunny, lovely place
Much better than the floor.

I waited till all was quiet –
In the middle of the night,
And made my way back to the door
From where I took my flight.

How cosy now I'm in my web,
And then I have to hope,
I won't be disturbed again
By that big black dope!

HYPOCRITE

She clutches her bible to her chest,
With its gold leafed edges.
She doesn't care about the rest
And all their worthless pledges.

She holds her bible very close,
A symbol oh so sacred.
Her hollow self – vacant, spinose
Self righteous in her head.

She champions her holy book
To excuse her own excesses.
At her own soul she never looks,
No truth as she confesses.

Her bible gives her credence,
Assured by her belief.
But she's a woman with no sense –
Be sure it leads to grief.

For all her worthless bible
Blinds her to the facts.
She lives by all its libel,
Imprudence she attracts.

With her good book she dances,
Believing all her lies.
She's thrown away her chances
For truth before she dies.

SACRIFIED

I feel the time creeping by
In my lonely room I sit,
Looking across at my TV
In this room so dimly lit.

I think about the life I've lived,
And what it's all been for.
If I could live it all again
Would I want some more?

The daily grind of 8 till 5
To keep them housed and fed,
And what the neighbours may think
And of anything they said.

All this stuff has brought me here
To this lonely place.
Across the room sitting there
Is that same old face.

She sits there silent
Just gazing at the wall.
Two people making loneliness
Listening to the rain fall.

In my once upon a time,
I was young and brash.
I was taking on the world,
Out there splashing cash.

I was eyeing up the girls,
Looking out for sex.
I was the toughest guy in town,
Where my muscles I would flex.

Then I came across this bird,
And suddenly I fell
Into this magic sort of trap,
Just like she'd cast a spell.

Then off we went – down the aisle,
As foolish as could be,
And onto the workforce treadmill
With no place for me to flee.

And so the years went racing by
With me wondering how
I wasted my life so shamefully
Considering my 'now'.

Not a word is spoken
As I look across the room.
Is her mind really blank
As she looks into the gloom?

A HOLE IN THE MOON

There came a time
When a rope led to the moon.
And mice, mice ran to and fro
Carrying cheese to the earth.
People devoured the cheese
And changed into human mountains
Who moved around on wheels.
More and more mice
Scurried up and down the rope,
Fetching cheese,
Transporting cheese,
Feeding cheese to human mountains
Who moved around on wheels.
Then the moon had a hole,
That gazed like an eye into space.
Still the mice fetched the cheese,
And the moon had many holes
Till it turned into a cheese ring
For the finger of fate.

A PIGEON CHASE AND PLACE

Once I had a silly job
In London town so fair.
I was young and foolish then
And didn't have a care.

When I'd finished work one day
And stepped into the street,
I met a lady clearly scared
Of the pigeons round her feet.

Her eyes were wide, her finger shook
As she pointed to the birds.
They milled around and billed and cooed,
'Twas all that could be heard.

"Will you try and help me please
To clear away this flock?
I just stood; they gathered round
And gave me such a shock!"

Ever willing to oblige,
I tipped my hat and said,
"I'll clap my hands and chase them off,
I'm sure that they'll be fled."

I clapped my hands and ran behind,
Assuming they would fly,
Instead they quickly ran in front,
I couldn't work out why.

So down the Strand I hurried on,
As more birds joined the group,
The lady followed in the rear
As I went in for the scoop.

I made a path for her to pass,
She said "Thanks," and hurried by.
We headed down to the Savoy –
I was sure that they would fly.

But on we rushed to the hotel
Where we entered in the foyer.
And there we met the maitre d'
Who wished us all "Good day."

"Do you have a booking, sir
For you and all your pets?
I take it you're here for the conference
That's been set up for Vets?"

The pigeons then were settled in
All sitting on their perches.
They really seemed to like it here –
Much better than the churches.

So now the birds all fitted up
So smart in bibs and tuckers.
All dwelling in the posh Savoy
In a life that's truly pukka!

TWO TRAVELLERS

Regret and Sadness
Ambled down the road,
To their crumbling folly
In illusory paradise.
Sadness stopped to weep
While Regret looked on,
Wondering how they could
So far have lost their way
On their road to nowhere.
A hooded jackdaw mocked them,
And a sprig of violet bella-donna
Bowed low at their coming.
"I can't go on. I can't go on,"
Wailed Sadness.
Regret shrugged.
"This is the only road;
The only way to go."
Two travellers
Going forward
Into the sunset.

THE WINGS OF BABY ROSIE

This room is quiet now,
Save for nearby weeping
And the silent penetration of sadness.
A cloth covers a small form –
A baby, with a slit in her throat.
The gasping has stopped;
The helpless glances passed around
Have been exchanged for sorrow.
Baby Rosie carried on the wings
Of diphtheria.
Her little brother too – Georgie
Now past redemption.
Empty arms.
And fear. Expectation – 'who's next?'

The boy lifted the cover
To see the face of his sister
Made angel.
He saw himself
Cradling and soothing her distress,
But his love was puny
Beside the mighty slayer
Who drained the breath from her tiny body.
He wept.
He thought of the time
When he had held her,
Transmitting his love
And will to live.
She was snatched from him
To die wretched
In case the evil assassin
Should extend a bony finger towards him.
Now she is still.
Baby Rosie.

BUTTERCUPS

The days were always hazy then.
The sun glimmered
As we lay in the yellow
Soothed in the sun.
We lived our contentment
Wrapped in goodness and love,
Shielding our eyes
In those bright, bright days of heaven
And perpetual summer
In our field of buttercups.

Then the heathens came –
And old age,
Crippled and implacable.
Waving a bony stick,
Forcing us to quit,
Forcing us apart.

Cold winds of winter
Decimated our buttercups,
And we lost each other in the maelstrom.

Now I think back to our buttercups
And I see a barren field.
Empty,
But for the fullness of winter.

ALL THAT REMAINS

When it is time to say goodbye,
When our paths divide.
When one, or both, are no more
Then just our love remains.

How will it be when one is left?
How will our severed world be then?
How will the key to life be found?
When all our love remains.

ASYLUM?

I want to watch your pixar.
I want to stand in my smart shirt
Watching the warm comfortable sunset.
I want to regard your worthless celebrities
In their glittering mansions
Their coffers full and overflowing.
And their luck ridden lives.

You came with your game-boy wars
To smash my region
And kill the despots
And leave me nothing.
My children drown in the Aegean
And my hands shake with cold
Over the fire built in shaped mud.

You argue over our numbers
And spread your hands helplessly,
"What to do! What to do!"
While we march to your razor wire
And our babies sleep in raw cold.
Are we not flesh and blood like you?
Should we pay for your retribution?

(Written 2016)

THE TRIP

You don't know me.
You have passed me on the street,
Feigning indifference,
Secretly disgusted - you hurry past.

I am caught on a hook of despair.
Imprisoned by a steel shot
That brings me salvation.

My arms are peppered with a thousand engorged dots
Now resisting more metal points.

Broken skin gleams like citrine
And ruby chippings.

My mind wants oblivion.
My body seeks the gasp
That buys the ticket to the magic ride.
It takes me up, up
To the land of nowhere,
But is so fleeting
I soon return to go

To tend to the wounded flesh of my hand
Butchered by injection.

TO NURSE A SNOWDROP

This lovely messenger of the Spring
Bows towards its snowy bed.
Plucked and placed
In a rusty vessel-
It seems to bend its head in shame.

This repository is perfectly honed
Designed with precise Germanic precision
The stem of the snowdrop leans
In fused ancient ashes
Which insult its standing.

Honed for war by Hitler's henchmen
Engineered for human mayhem -
It fell in a London street,
With fiery explosive trail,
To kill and maim all in its path.

It is quiet now;
Content to contain the peace of the snowdrop.
How many lives did it extinguish in its wake
Before it changed to a piece of rusty shrapnel
Nursing a snowdrop?

THE GIFT

What's happened to me,
Am I really so mad?
I want to go back
And re-live what I had.

Life was so simple,
The whole world was mine!
My relatives all there,
It was really divine.

My figure was gorgeous,
I was so young.
The music around me
Were all the best songs.

Conversations were lively -
Good always to meet
And listen to others;
Attitudes were sweet.

And we could laugh
At anything; at everything
And never worry
If it were cursed with a sting.

We watched telly together,
As we sat round the box.
Some would eat crisps
While others munched chocs.

We'd gather as families
Glad to be together.
It seemed that those times
Would go on forever.

Then we were gifted -
By Tim Burners-Lee,
The sublimity of internet.
What a catastrophe!

The world was subsumed
By a practice so strange,
In just a short time
It had rattled our brains.

People got wired
And they listened alone.
They walked down the street
And talked to their phone.

They shut all the shops,
And with just a click
They buy what they like,
Ghost streets endemic.

To get a message across
They now send a text,
If that doesn't work
Then Facebook is next.

See all the friends they have -
Though they've never met.
They rely on these mates -
They're not seen as a threat…

This grand communication
Seems to be just what they need,
It feeds their depression,
The alarms they don't heed.

Now all of these changes -
It's just how it is.
Now the old life is past
Along with its riches.

STRANGE MR SANDERS

Deserted street. Just me here.
The gathering dark. The cold –
I quicken my step. It's clear
I must hurry to a place
Where I can leave behind distress.
I don't look back, just on
Into a time of fortune, lest
I fall again to despair.
Ah, here is the door. I knock
"Oh, Mr Sanders. I have your room.
No luggage? No. Key's in the lock."
I see her puzzlement. Feel her mind.
"I've come to sell my stamps,
They're in my briefcases,
Look. Here, under the lamp."
She stares in wonderment.
My only treasures – the last
Of my worldly goods, the rest -
Dissolved in bankruptcy in the past.
Stolen, taken by a twist of fate.

SO STRANGE...

He carried two brief cases
Of tanned hide leather.
He came to my door
And asked whether
I could offer him lodgings –
For a couple of nights,
So he could take his collection
And maybe he might
Redeem his stamp stash
To realise some wealth.
He knew well his business
And must rely on stealth.
Why was he pitched into indigence?
Life had become his controller.
This smartly dressed man –
Who tipped his bowler
With such sophistication.
He would try to arrange
A good sale for his stamps,
But he seemed so strange…

WHEN SANTA GOT WAYLAID

The sleigh sat trembling in the air
Packed with sacks and children's ware.
Waiting in the swirling snow
For Santa Claus, and then to go –

Chasing off across the roof tops,
Making all the familiar stops.
Leaving dolls and planes and toys
For the sleeping girls and boys.

In this dash across the town,
They see Coco the circus clown.
He's wandering aimlessly about
And then they think they hear him shout…

"Wait for me, with your busy sleigh
I have nothing to do today.
I could help you deliver your load
To the children in this road."

"Shhh," cried Santa. "Don't you know
A circus clown just cannot go
And deliver presents here and there –
It's Santa's job, and isn't fair.

Where's your circus, and all your friends?"
"I've lost my way, I can't pretend
I stayed too late in the inn
Drinking large amounts of gin.

But now I've sobered up I think,
I won't be having another drink.
I'd like to help you with your sack,
Look – I've got a good strong back."

Santa Claus was very cross,
On Christmas Eve he was boss.
He couldn't waste time standing here,
His annoyance then he made clear.

"The children out there, sleeping now,
Will wake tomorrow wondering how
All their presents and their gifts
Are scattered in the deep snowdrifts.

'Cause this is what I truly think.
If you believe that you can drink
And then to come and be some use –
You really are a silly goose!

Come, hop aboard my busy sleigh,
I'll take you off, and on my way
To Alcoholics Anonymous we will go,
The perfect place for such a hobo!"

And on arrival they were shut,
So Coco remained and looked half cut.
And Santa continued on his way
And thought, "I shall regret this day."

At the next stop Santa saw
A notice fixed upon the door –
'Take a mince pie and glass of sherry,
We hope all your Christmases will be merry.'

Santa quickly hustled in
And put the mince pies in the bin.
Then taking the sherry to the sink
Tipped away poor Coco's drink.

Coco helped pile presents high
And looked at Santa very sly –
For there behind the kitchen door
Were alcoholic drinks galore.

Into his pockets wide and deep
He placed some bottles there to keep,
To help himself when the need arose
Then Santa said, "Don't touch those."

"No, no, dear Santa, I wouldn't dare
To touch those drinks placed down there.
What a dismal thing to do
To take more drink and upset you

On such a night and busy time,
To get more drunk would be a crime."
"Yes, it would. Now quickly on
It's getting late we must be gone."

To the sleigh they quickly scurried
Then to the next call the reindeers hurried.
But Coco's reluctance to leave the sleigh
As well as his tilted blue toupee –

Made Santa cross when he heard
The chink of bottles – but undeterred
He continued delivering fast as light,
Dashing quickly through the night.

Coco continued in his seat
And gulped down all the spirits neat.
The more he took the more he swayed
Then Santa said, "I am afraid

I cannot take you back with me
To Toyland. It would surely be
The greatest travesty of trust.
I'll leave you here and then I must

Get back quickly because the light
Will be returning, and I might
Be spotted by a waking boy,
My cover blown because your ploy

To get so drunk and mess things up.
So clear off before I string you up!"
Coco wobbled to the ground,
And Santa left without a sound.

Then Coco stumbled to a house
Making merry and loud carouse.
When in the street he did espy
An angry parent who gave a sigh.

"Now tell me, what you doing here?
Partaking of your Christmas cheer.
With noises fit to wake the dead,
And getting people out of bed.

It's Christmas day! You surely know
Good will to men, and lots of snow…"
At this point down poor Coco fell
Though being drunk they could not tell.

And so we leave him lying there
In the Christmas snow, to swear
He'd been with Santa all that night
In the sky and bright starlight.

When he sobers up on Boxing day
People in disbelief will say,
"You were drunk and could not have been
With Santa – he is never seen."

Only the family without their booze
Dull sobriety they did not choose.
'Cause they think Santa pinched their stuff
And cause of Coco their Noel was duff!

CHRISTMAS TREE

A
tree
glittery
for Christmas.
Children watching,
With eager smiling faces
Waiting for the magical night.
This is Santa's big scene.
The tree with all it's colours,
Must be right for it's Yuletide visitor.
Glass of sherry, mince pie,
Dance attendance on the tree.
The children climb the stairs for bed.
The trees glittery lights
Wink happily in the darkness,
As a man in red opens a bulging sack,
Overflowing with gifts,
For children sleeping soundly
Soon to find presents piled by Santa.
Softly,
Quietly
Rising at the crack of dawn,
Bleary eyed children
Squeal with joy,
"He's been."
"He's been."

TO AN ELDERFLOWER

I see a wedding in the elderflower.
Delicate white and cream petals
With tiny bud balls
To decorate the silky hair of the bride
with a trinket tiara from nature.
It seems to represent
                  ballet dancing gaiety,
and has a soft surety
of charming importance.
A circlet of pollen filled pale saffron
                    for a fairy bride.
But for now
It sits on the tree,
Advertising its prettiness
as it shifts in the breeze.
Immature companions
Sit at either side
Unopened, green and indifferent,
Waiting for the sun and rain
To change them
To fitting bubbly companions
for their elder sister.

STONE OF SISYPHUS

I am the stone of Sisyphus.
I ponder my crime, each time
The perpetual struggle for triumph fails.
It breaks my soul to roll down and down
While my tormentor cheerfully –
With the weight of the punishment
On his shoulder – strains the boulder
To his willing will.
Again he will try – Oh hear my cry!
For my brothers lie at rest.
Only the juggling sea
Serves as their persecutor.
Their fate to sleep in comfort
In their Procrustean bed,
While my sin is my circle,
My strong back and weak mind.
My existence resile, servile, futile.

PINK CLOUDS

Pink clouds were weeping,
Keeping lots of pots of dye
To try to change their hue
To blue, but knew
The sky was dyed azure for sure
So no changed was possible
Yet.

Printed in Great Britain
by Amazon

27189253R00050